The Courageous Conversations at Work Series

DEALING WITH A DIFFICULT CO-WORKER

VOLUME ONE

DAVID LEE

Legal and Copyright

For permission requests, write to the publisher at the following email:
Info@HumanNatureAtWork.com

Ordering Information:
Quantity sales. Special discounts are available on quantity purchases by corporations, associations, and others. For details, contact the publisher at the above email or go to: HumanNatureAtWork.com

For Interviews, email:
David@HumanNatureAtWork.com

Printed in the United States of America
First Edition
ISBN 978-1-0865-7241-4

Contents

Section One

Section Two

Section Three

About This Series

Challenging a Difficult Co-Worker is the first volume of the *Courageous Conversations at Work* series. Each book will be based on a single story involving a challenging workplace conversation.

These "little books with big lessons" are designed to be useful whether you simply read them on your own, or if they are used as the foundation of a seminar conducted in your organization.

The lessons contained in this and future *Courageous Conversations at Work* books are delivered within the context of a story -- because stories are more interesting and memorable than teaching methods reliant on traditional academic lectures. Lisa Cron, author of *Wired for Story: The Writer's Guide to Using Brain Science to Hook Readers from the Very First Sentence*, writes that stories translate "big ideas, abstract concepts, dry facts" into relatable experiences.

The term "experience" is key to understanding why learning through stories is so powerful.

The VitalSmarts team, authors of *Influencer: The New Science of Leading Change*, explain the power of storytelling in the following way: They note that experience is the best teacher, while vicarious experience is the second best teacher. Watching someone or hearing about them doing something (if told well) creates an imaginedexperiencewhere you are putting yourself in their shoes. You empathize with what they are feeling, and you are envisioning engaging in the experience that they are having. It's like when athletes visualize themselves performing with perfection. Their brain is experiencing their visualization as if it were actually happening.

Another way of thinking about why you want to learn via stories comes from the wonderful book *Made to Stick: Why Some Ideas Survive and Others Die* by Chip and Dan Heath. They identify six characteristics of communication that is "sticky." One of those characteristics is telling through stories. The brothers Heath phrase it so perfectly when they write that stories "provide both inspiration and simulation."

In other words, let's say you hear a story about someone facing their fears and having a courageous conversation, and the story includes the whole picture. How they went through the process of overcoming their fear of confronting the other person, how they shifted into a positive, empowered state,how they brought up the issue to the person, and then how it worked out.

When you hear (or in this case, read) the story, not only does it give you hope that you can do that too—i.e. it provides inspiration—it also acts as a simulation, like flight simulators do for pilots, or like a training video does.

So stories of people facing and overcoming challenges not only create a vision of what is possible and give us hope, they also show us how we can do that ourselves.

So...that's why the guiding principles and techniques illustrated in this book are brought to you in a story.

Something you'll notice about how I tell the story in this book is that I don't simply share what happened and what I and the other person said.

I also share a lot of my interior world, my thoughts and feelings. My intention in doing that is to help you identify your own thoughts, feelings, and reactions related to difficult conversations you've had or know you need to have.

I've found over the years that it's extremely useful to recognize what we are thinking and feeling in response to another's words or behaviors, because our thoughts and feelings have a huge impact on how we "show up" when we have the conversation.

Another way of saying this is "it's the meaning we make, not the actual situation that determines our reaction to it."

Let's say you go into a conversation thinking: "She said that just to get back at me!" or "I know she's going to get really defensive when I bring it up…I know it's going to be a disaster."

If that's how you explain to yourself why she said what she did, and if that's what you believe she will do when you try to talk to her about what she said, you are likely to enter the conversation feeling angry and anxious.

Conversely, let's say you go into the conversation having made the following meaning out of what she had said: "I don't know why she said that. Maybe she was feeling overwhelmed. Maybe she was having a bad day. I don't know."

Think of the different emotions that meaning creates.

Now, let's say you have the following thought about the upcoming conversation: "I don't know why she said it, so I'll give her the benefit of the doubt and do my best to bring it up in a low-key, friendly way. I'll make sure I enter the conversation truly trying to understand where she was coming from."

Think of the difference that self-talk would make on how you felt and acted when you brought up the issue, compared to thinking: "I know she's going to get really defensive when I bring it up…I know it's going to be a disaster."

That's why it's so important to become aware of our self-talk, and the meaning we make of a situation, and then, being able to challenge unproductive self-talk and explanations we tell ourselves.

So, with that in mind, as you read this story—and future ones in the series—please use my sharing of self-talk and explanations I engaged in as a launch pad to examine *your* self-talk and explanations. We will explore later on in the story why this is so important; for now, I just want to say this:

Your ability to identify and challenge counterproductive self-talk and explanations for others' behaviors hugely impacts your ability to bring your best self to a courageous conversation -- and increases the odds that your conversation will go well.

Introduction

I'm excited to share the knowledge contained in this story with you because of the difference it can make in your life and—if you bring this into your workplace—the difference it can make to your employer.

I say this based on both my personal experience working on developing my skills at bringing up and discussing difficult issues, as well as the work I've done over the years as a coach, consultant, and trainer.

The Difference It Can Make In Your Life

Your ability to bring up important, difficult issues and engage people in constructive conversations around them has an enormous influence on:

Your overall happiness—Think of people in your life with whom you have unresolved conflict, or with whom there is ongoing tension in your interactions. Think of how that affects you. Conversely, think of how you feel when you are able to work things out with people, and the sense of peace you feel, compared to the nagging unease you feel when there's strain between you and others.

Your overall stress level—For most people, the major source of workplace stress comes from interactions with others, whether with their co-workers or their supervisor. Think about your own experience over the years. When you think of days you leave work feeling drained, isn't it more often due to unpleasant interactions with others rather than the technical demands of your work?

Your effectiveness in your job, and therefore your job security—Your ability to get results in your job depends in large part on your ability to work well with others. It depends on your ability to "get results through other people" as the saying goes. Therefore, the more skilled you are at engaging people in productive conversations, especially around difficult and important issues, the more effective you will be. Thus, your value as an employee, and therefore your level of job security, is closely tied to this skill set.

Your career trajectory—The higher a person rises in leadership, the more skilled they need to be in addressing difficult issues, dealing effectively with strong personalities, navigating complex interpersonal terrain, delivering difficult messages, and getting buy-in. Learning how to have these and other challenging conversations can make a big difference in your ability to advance in your career towards increasingly higher leadership positions.

The Difference It Can Make To Your Employer

Imagine the difference it would make in an organization if people consistently discussed issues getting in the way of them working well together, or getting the results they want, rather than react in these common ways:

1. **Remain silent while becoming increasingly more frustrated and resentful.** Some people stay silent until they've "had it up to here" and then blow up, often saying things that don't accurately or coherently communicate why they're upset, and often

saying things they later regret. Other people vent their anger and frustration to coworkers, spreading negativity.

2. **Engage in "payback behaviors."** These could be sarcastic digs, sniping in meetings, not responding promptly to the other person's emails, withholding information and support out of spite, and all the other passive-aggressive and just plain aggressive behaviors we engage in when we are upset with others but aren't willing or able to talk about why we're upset.

3. **Avoid interacting with the other person.** Rather than deal with the discomfort of interacting with the person, sometimes we simply avoid them at all costs, including situations where they would be the natural "go to" person for information or support.

Consider times you've either engaged in any of these reactions or witnessed them among your team members or other colleagues. Then think of the cost to your employer when employees do these things rather than talk through conflict, or raise important and difficult-to-talk-about issues.

Here's a partial list of the price organizations pay when people are not willing or able to bring up difficult issues and have courageous conversations:

Increased turnover and decreased engagement—When employees and their supervisors don't have the skills to talk about issues causing that employee's performance and engagement to diminish, one of two things will happen.

First, that employee is probably going to leave. Second, if they do stay, they will be among the ROAD Warriors that comprise the majority of the US workforce, according to Gallup's research.

Gallup refers to employees who are disengaged as Retired On Active Duty. They are the more than half the workforce who have "unofficially retired," despite continuing to show up at work and collect a paycheck.

While their body shows up, their heart and mind do not.

It isn't just the supervisor/employee relationship that requires courage and candor. Senior leadership needs to engage employees in candid conversations around morale issues, rather than hope their "Well it is what it is…they just need to deal with it" attitude will result in employees accepting whatever edicts senior leadership hands down.

When senior leadership engages in communication practices that foster psychological safety and welcome unguarded honesty, they make it possible to get the information they need to keep morale high during difficult times, become an Employer of Choice for talent, and create a work environment that brings out the best in their employees.

Increased Accidents and Injuries, and Other Safety-Related Costs— A "safety culture" depends on employees feeling empowered to speak up when they see unsafe practices, and feeling like they can report accidents and injuries without creating problems for themselves.

When they don't feel psychologically safe to do so, employees put themselves and others at risk, and are likely to cost their employer in terms of workers compensation claims and other safety-related costs.

Resistance To Change Initiatives, Process Improvements, And Product Rollouts (especially those with aggressive deadlines)—If employees don't feel safe enough or skilled enough to voice their concerns effectively, they are likely to silently resist organizational changes and product rollouts they have concerns about. Given the realities of accelerating change in today's world, and the need for a nimble, agile response by organizations, employee resistance to change and strategy execution carries with it a steep price. Knowing how to create a climate where employees are willing to share their concerns—rather than act them out through sabotage—makes a huge difference in leadership's ability to both get buy-in and get valuable "in the trenches" feedback that can help them improve on their initial execution strategy.

Where This Comes From and What That Has to Do With You

I'm Probably No Different from You

When I give presentations on courageous conversations, I emphasize to participants that I am probably as conflict-averse as they are, and that I also suffer from "delayed intelligence." That's the frustrating phenomenon of being able to come up with witty comebacks hours, days, or weeks too late.

I share that with audiences because I don't want them to discount what I'm saying based on assuming courageous conversations areeasy for me or come naturally.

I remember attending a conference presentation by the author of an outstanding book on how to deal with difficult people. I recall loving his presentation and being really impressed with himand his quick wit. I also remember thinking "His approach comes naturally to him because of his quick wit. That's not who I am."

Looking back on my reaction, I believe it was partially true. Based on his style of communication, it was clear this person was very quick witted, seemed to enjoy banter, and could clearly hold his own in conversations.

What was probably *not* true was that he had always been good at addressing difficult people.

That probably was *not* the case.

While by nature he was incredibly clever and seemed like the kind of personality that might even enjoy mixing it up with people, I'm sure his confidence had increased over time as his ability had increased through learning and practice.

I think that's important to keep in mind as you read this story because I don't want you to shortchange yourself by thinking "Oh…he could have that conversation (and other difficult conversations) because it's easy for him. That won't work for me."

Believe me, even though I consider myself and expert on the subject, having those conversations is NOT easy for me.

I share that with you because I want you to know that I am not someone who is unaffected by conflict or other people's anger, like some people seem to be, and that bringing up difficult issues still isn't easy for me.

But I still do it.

And it becomes easier each time I do.

Speaking From Experience...

Part of why I'm so passionate about courageous conversation skills is because of the difference they have made in my life.

While I still find disagreement and conflict uncomfortable, I am much more likely to bring up what needs to be talked about than stay silent and let resentment grow or have the issue create distance in a relationship.

I have had conversations over the years where I wasn't optimistic that the other person would be able to engage in a mature, productive conversation, but…because I did my "homework" ahead of time, I was able to show up for the conversation in a non-combative, open-minded, positive (or at least neutral) emotional state, and phrase my request to discuss the issue in a way that elicited a positive response .

Because I had done the work ahead of time, and I had developed the skills through years of practice, we were able to have an open-minded, open-hearted conversation that resolved the issue.

Each time I experience a successful courageous conversation, I am reminded that you never know what a person is capable of when it comes to engaging in a healthy, mature conversation -- until you give them a chance.

For me, that's a message of hope each time I consider whether I want to bring up a difficult issue with someone I experience as immature or primitive in their way of relating.

Because you just never know until you try.

So, everything I teach, and will share with you in the upcoming story, comes from hard work in real world encounters, and applies what I've learned from many different sources.

On the professional level, my work in this area has been informed by my first career as a counselor, and my current work as a consultant, trainer, and executive coach, where much of my work has focused on this question: "How do you have the conversations necessary to get the results you need to get and build the relationships you need to build?"

How to Make the Most of This

Prime Your Brain

There's a term in neuroscience called "priming" which you can use here and in any learning context. It helps your brain notice information in learning contexts and connect it to situations in your life where you could benefit most from applying that information.

That source of all knowledge in today's world—Wikipedia—describes priming as: "...a technique whereby exposure to one stimulus influences a response to a subsequent stimulus, without conscious guidance or intention. For example, the word NURSE is recognized more quickly following the word DOCTOR than following the word BREAD."

You can prime your brain to pick up on ideas that will be most helpful to you by thinking right now of some of the challenging conversations you need to have and difficult ones you've had that didn't work out well.

This activates your brain—i.e. it primes your brain—to pick up on points that could be helpful in those situations.

Use This as Your Own Personal Workshop

You can benefit from reading this story "as is," but you will get the greatest benefit if you use it as a framework to learn and apply the courageous conversation guiding principles and skills I teach in seminars.

You can turn this into your own individual workshop by downloading the courageous conversations worksheet at humannatureatwork.com/cc-worksheet.

This will help you translate what is covered in this book into the conversations you need to have, and by doing so, enable this story to make a much bigger difference in your life.

Use This to Facilitate In-House Seminars

You can use this story as the foundation for a one to three hour in-house seminar. For this, each participant would have their own copy of this book, and you can email me at david@humannatureatwork.com about how to get the facilitator's guide and workbooks for participants.

Use This Again and Again

One of my favorite sayings when it comes to these skills is "School is never out."

Becoming skilled at engaging people in constructive conversations around important issues is a never-ending learning process. It's sort of like a martial art. Masters in the martial arts never stop practicing the fundamentals. They know the more solid their understanding of the fundamentals, the greater their ability to adapt to any situation.

They know that that each person they spar with provides them with the opportunity to grow their skills, develop greater adaptability, and cultivate their capacity to remain centered, despite how challenging the situation.

Now, I want to be clear that my using this metaphor does not mean I see engaging people in courageous conversations as a battle, it's just an easy-to-understand analogy for why we need to continue to learn and practice, and not think because we read a book or went to a seminar, that we should be skilled, or that it should be easy.

In fact, even though I have taught and coached people in this area for twenty years, I still reach out to close friends who are either counselors, psychologists, or coaches to get their perspective when I'm struggling with how to best address a challenging interpersonal situation.

I know that because I'm in the midst of a situation, and therefore emotionally involved, there are things I don't see, or don't see accurately, that a wise, skilled, dispassionate person can.

One of these people is my close friend Fran Liautaud, who is a world class coach who helps people engage in "fierce conversations." She is a master at asking questions that result in a complete shift in how you see and feel about a situation. Over the years when I've felt stuck on how to deal with a situation, Fran will ask just the right question to help me get unstuck. Conversely, other times Fran has felt stuck and come to me, and through our conversation, she's become unstuck.

I share this to emphasize that "school is never out" no matter how skilled you are. With Fran and me, you have two people who teach these skills, coach others in how to have these conversations, and who walk our talk, and...we still at times need outside help.

Thus, I hope you revisit this story over the years and use the support materials to help you continue to develop your ability to engage people in courageous conversations.

And now…our story…

Did He Really Just Say That?

I had been working at my new employer, an insurance company, for a couple of months when I noticed how one of my fellow managers, who I'll call Sam, often acted strangely in meetings.

Sam would make unprofessional, inappropriate, and just plain weird comments to colleagues in meetings when he disagreed with them. His verbal attacks were what you might expect from a middle school or junior high boy, not a thirtysomething professional.

I was stunned by Sam's behavior. Being new to this company and new to a corporate environment, I wasn't sure what to make of it.

Was this considered acceptable behavior?

Was this a cultural norm?

After a couple of months on the job, I got to be the target of Sam's in-your-face humor.

We were in a problem-solving meeting and I offered up an idea.

After I finished, Sam blurted out: "That idea stinks…and so do you."

I was stunned.

I had no idea what to say to that.

How does one respond to such a strange combination of the rude and the ridiculous?

Do you confront the person and let them know they crossed a line or do you let it go and not dignify the comment with a reply?

In reality, even if I had decided to challenge Sam, I wouldn't have known what to say, because I have "delayed intelligence."

You might be able to relate. That's when you come up with a witty retort, except it's hours or days too late.

When the meeting was over, I returned to my office and sat down at my desk.

Guess what I started to do.

Did I review my To Do List? Did I dive into my work?

Of course not.

I did what most of us do in situations like these. I replayed the scenario with Sam over and over, berating myself for not having a witty retort that would have put Sam in his place.

I interspersed my self-flagellation with statements about what a jerk Sam was and how his behavior was horrible and inexcusable:

I quickly worked myself into a state of self-righteous outrage with self-talk like:

> *"How dare he talk to me that way!"*

"Who does he think he is?"

"What makes him think it's OK to treat people like that?"

"What a jerk!" (actually that's a workplace-friendly version of what I said)

From Ruminating to Plotting Revenge

After repeatedly replaying the Sam scenario in my mind, complete with self-righteous outrage commentary, my energy for doing so started to abate.

I found it harder to muster the energy to be outraged.

In fact, I started to feel a bit bored with it all.

I was certain in my belief that Sam was a jerk and he shouldn't act that way.

I was also still angry with myself for not knowing how I should have responded.

Not wanting to be caught unprepared again, I started thinking about what I would say if Sam ever said that again.

Fortunately, it didn't take long for me to come to my senses and recognize that Sam was unlikely to say the EXACT same thing, so planning responses to that comment was a waste of time.

My thought-process sharpened by this realization, I shifted to the next logical agenda: think up a putdown that would let Sam know it would be a mistake to mess with me again.

In other words, I started channeling my inner adolescent.

“That’s the ticket,” I thought, feeling a surge of efficacy, feeling good that I now had the beginnings of a plan, “I’ll go for a preemptive strike that punishes him for what he did to me *and* lets him know it’s not wise to mess with me.”

It was a brilliant twofer, I concluded.

Coming to My Senses

Fortunately, after wasting less than an hour on this strategy, I realized it would be a major mistake.

Trying to teach Sam a lesson by delivering a crushing putdown was like the old adage: "Never bring a knife to a gun fight."

Sam had demonstrated he was very skilled at put downs and verbal fighting.

I am good at neither.

I realized I could spend hours crafting the perfect put down and with his skill level, he could easily come up with a retort that would crush my putdown, which would leave me once again feeling angry and outraged. So why waste my time trying to come up with the ultimate putdown?

Oh...and There's the Whole "Walk Your Talk" Thing

My second "Ah hah" was more sobering.

Ah…wait a minute, here, I thought, remember how you teach people about addressing issues directly rather than getting your point across in sarcastic, passive-aggressive or other antagonistic ways? Since you believe in walking your talk, there's no way you can be working on playing mind games and planning for verbal sparring matches with Sam, and still feel good about yourself. You would not be practicing what you preach.

Chastened by this realization, I decided I would take the High Road and shift my attention to how I could address the issue directly.

So What Does "Address an Issue Directly" Actually Look Like?

My decision to address the problem with Sam directly brought with it a whole new set of challenges and fears.

At the simplest level, it brought up this question:

"What would addressing the issue directly sound like?"

How could I say directly and clearly what I needed to say without doing so in an overly intense, judgmental, or aggressive way?

How could I be candid and direct in a way that wouldn't automatically trigger defensiveness and antagonism?

My dilemma at this point speaks to a challenge we all face when we choose to confront someone about something they did or said. It's especially difficult when that person has historically been unpleasant, or demonstrated an unwillingness or inability to talk maturely about difficult issues.

How direct and unfiltered should you be?

How much should you share about how they've affected you, and how vulnerable should you be about how you feel?

One answer to these questions comes from Dr. Angeles Arrien's admonition to "Speak your truth without blame or judgment."

Speaking your truth means sharing your experience. It's coming from a place of: *This is what it was like for me.*

Notice that sharing your experience and perspective is about YOU, not about the other person and your evaluation of them.

In this situation, my "experience" was one of feeling shocked and angry over Sam talking to me—or anyone else for that matter—in the way he did.

What Do I Share And What Do I NOT Share?

Now that I had decided to talk with Sam directly, I started to wrestle with an important issue in these types of situations: how much should I share about my reaction?

How candid should I be?

How vulnerable should I be?

Should I let Sam know that his remarks had bothered me?

Since Sam had repeatedly demonstrated junior high level maturity in his verbal attacks on others, I could easily imagine that Sam would enjoy hearing this, and such an admission would give him incentive to do more of the same.

Finding the Right Degree of Vulnerability

I was clear, given Sam's pattern of disrespectful interactions with others, that I didn't want to make myself as transparent or vulnerable as I would to a friend with whom I felt emotionally safe.

With a close friend, I might have said:

"Hey…I wanted to talk with you about what you said to me in the meeting yesterday. I was really hurt that you would say that to me and especially in front of others….what was up with that?"

With a friend, I would be comfortable being that open and real, because I wouldn't choose someone to be a friend if they shamed people or used what someone shared against them in the future.

Since Sam wasn't a friend, and since he hadn't shown any indication he would treat my vulnerability with respect, I did not want to use such a vulnerable approach.

Also, in actuality, I didn't feel hurt by Sam's behavior. Because Sam's comments were so juvenile, I didn't feel hurt as I probably would have if Sam had made some disparaging remark that had some validity, or wasn't so ridiculous. In this case, I felt more anger and outrage that a person would treat *anyone* so disrespectfully.

"OK…I'm not going to share THAT, but what DO I share?"

At this point, I had moved along in the process from what I knew I didn't want to share, to wondering what exactly I DID want to.

The first alternative that popped into my head seemed to come from my Inner Adolescent.

I considered using "humor" by saying something like "Hey Sam…you were kind of a jerk in yesterday's meeting…what was up with THAT?" in a joking tone of voice.

Fortunately, I quickly dismissed that brilliant idea.

Clearly that sarcastic approach would have triggered antagonism, or, at the very least, Sam would have responded to my sarcasm with his own. He certainly would not have said "Oh...you're right...I was being a jerk...thanks for pointing that out. I'm really sorry."

So What IS "Just Right"?

Fortunately, I was able to corral my adolescent self and recognize how immature and unproductive that opener would be as a conversation starter.

As I came to my senses, I felt humbled by how easy it was to consider such an immature approach despite years of professionally strategizing how to bring up difficult issues in a mature, respectful way. It was a useful reminder that can help me be more compassionate when I think someone is acting immaturely.

At this stage in my thought process, I had reached the Goldilocks Decision.

My natural response was "too vulnerable" for the situation, while the alternative approach swung too far in the opposite direction and was "too aggressive," and just plain immature.

So, what response would be neither too vulnerable nor too aggressive, but rather, "just right"? I wondered.

How could I practice "speak your truth without blame or judgment" as Dr. Angeles Arrien used to teach?

How could I share my experience of what happened, and request that Sam NOT do it again without my authentic sharing becoming an invitation for Sam to do more of the same?

What's The Outcome I Desire?

In trying to figure this out, I asked a question that's important to ask when considering how to bring up an issue.

That question is "What's the outcome I desire?"

Asking this helps guide us in choosing the words we use.

Asking "Does what I'm thinking of saying help me achieve my outcome?" is a useful reality check.

Asking what outcome we want to achieve also helps us and dispel outcomes we fantasize about that are not productive or unrealistic.

Unearthing unproductive and unrealistic desired outcomes helps us avoid spending time on creating a great strategy to achieve a goal that would hurt us in the end, or trying to figure out a strategy to achieve a goal that is unachievable.

Here are some examples of undesirable or unattainable outcomes:

1. **Showing the person why they are so incredibly wrong or bad because of what they did.**—Even if we believe this to be true, most people don't appreciate these messages, and tend to respond in defensive, combative ways.

2. **Trying to punish the person.**—This is when we hope our bringing up the issue or giving them feedback will make them feel bad, as payback for the pain we felt over their behavior. While doing this might bring short-term relief—e.g. the "joy of telling someone off"—the negative consequences are both obvious and potentially devastating both in immediate and long-lasting consequences.

3. **Trying to change the person's core personality.**—While I think it's useful to give people feedback—if done skillfully and if they are open to it—we also need to ask ourselves if we are trying to get someone to change their fundamental personality. So for instance, if someone tends to be very direct, blunt, and often harsh, you might be able to get them to become more mindful of their style and soften a bit in their interaction with you, but their innate personality will continue to drive their style of relating.

Transforming a Counterproductive Outcome Intention to a Productive One

While I was in my angry, outraged state, my initial inclination was to punish Sam.

I wanted him to feel as uncomfortable as I had when Sam made his rude remarks.

I wanted Sam to squirm as he saw the error of his ways.

Fortunately, I got a grip and could see that these self-serving wishes were unproductive.

I got to this more rational place, in part, because I reached out to my wise friend Bonnie, and vented, which discharged much of my pent-up anger.

After much venting and processing, I finally got to the place where I was ready to look at the situation in a fairly calm, reasonable state. I was finally able to get to a place of being truly interested in hearing where he was coming from rather than simply telling him off.

I had finally reached the state of being "curious, not furious."

From Furious to Curious

Shifting from Furious to Curious is one of THE most effective strategies for shifting our emotional state to one that not only feels better, but also allows us to think more clearly and rationally.

When we're in a state of curiosity, we can't be indignant and self-righteous – because curiosity is just not conducive to those emotions.

When we're feeling curious—and not furious—we are in a strong, alive, forward-thinking, wide open emotional and mental state that facilitates the discovery of optimal solutions.

In this state of curiosity, we're not going off on internal rants filled with "How dare he…!!!!" and "Who does she think she is!!!!"

Instead, we are wondering "Hmmm…what would be an effective way to deal with this?" or "What might be a good way to bring this up?"

So, thankfully, I was able to finally get into a state of curiosity by using the strategies I mentioned.

One in a state of curiosity, my anger disappeared and was replaced with an energized, yet peaceful state.

I found myself eager to find out what had motivated Sam to say what he did.

I felt ready for the challenge of having the conversation.

In this new, more resourceful state, my initial goal of wanting to punish Sam shifted to these objectives:

1. To engage Sam in a respectful conversation so that Sam could hear what I had to say without Sam feeling attacked and getting defensive.

2. To understand where Sam was coming from when he made his remarks.

3. For Sam to never talk to me that way again.

These objectives were reasonable, achievable, and positive. There was no vengeful or mean-spirited motivation behind them.

Now that I was clear on the outcomes I wanted, the next question was "OK…now…how do I make that happen?"

Starting the Conversation Off on the Right Foot

The way we start off a courageous conversation can make or break the conversation.

The words we use and the attitude and emotional state we enter into it with can either result in triggering a defensive, angry, combative response in the other person or foster a productive conversation.

If we go in with an angry accusatory attitude and bring up the issue in a clumsy, antagonistic manner, the other person is likely to feel threatened, and become defensive or combative. In that state, their response will be unproductive. Trying to shift someone from defensive and combative to open-minded, open-hearted, and rational is very difficult. It's MUCH easier to keep a conversation going in a productive direction, than it is to get it back on track.

Thus, it's so important to think through carefully how we want to start off the conversation, so we increase the odds that the person will remain in a positive emotional and mental state, and be capable of a productive conversation.

I like to describe the opening of the conversation as the Declaration/ Invitation process. The simple rhyme will hopefully make it easy to remember the two step process and the goal of each step.

In the Declaration, we "declare" what we want to talk about.

In the Invitation, we "invite" the person into a dialogue.

Here's how it works…

The Declaration

The goal of the Declaration step is to clearly and concisely describe what you want to talk about in a way that fosters receptivity.

When formulating your Declaration, here are questions to ask yourself:

1. **How can I make my point with as few words as possible**?--You want to use just enough words to make it clear what you want to talk about. You don't want to go on and on, which can create the feeling of being talked at or lectured to—neither being a pleasant experience, and neither likely to elicit a pleasant response.

   Talking at someone or sounding like we are lecturing can trigger defensiveness, because it replicates adult/child interactions most of us despised as children.

   We've all had that frustrating—and at times, infuriating—experience of having an adult, whether teacher, principal, or parent, going on and on about something we did wrong, while we had to sit in silence.

   When someone delivers a long-winded monologue about what we did that made them unhappy, not only does it replicate the "adult scolding the kid" dynamic from childhood, it also gets tedious and frustrating for the listener, especially if they grasped the message in the first few sentences.

Thus, with the Declaration, the goal is "Use only enough words to make your point and no more."

2. **What is the least forceful, least intense way of getting my point across, while still maintaining the integrity of my message?**—There is an old Chinese proverb that goes: "Do not remove a fly from your friend's forehead with a hatchet." Another pithy saying I heard years ago was "Don't go rabbit hunting with an elephant gun." While both metaphors are a bit grisly, they are good reminders not to overdo the intensity when bringing up a difficult issue. The more forceful and intense we are in getting our point across, the more likely we will trigger a defensive or antagonistic response.

   Thus, I almost always advocate using a light touch at the beginning.

   As the conversation progresses, we might realize our light touch hasn't registered; they don't seem to be getting the seriousness or importance of what we are saying. If that happens, we can always dial up the intensity.

The Invitation

Once you have declared what it is you want to talk about, the next step is to invite them into a conversation about this topic.

The goal of the invitation is to make our request as inviting as possible.

We want to make it clear we want to engage in a dialogue, that we are open to hearing their point of view, and that it is safe for them to be candid and unguarded with us.

The invitation can involve you asking for:

1. Their point of view
2. Their reaction to what you just said.
3. Them to answer a question you just raised.
4. Them to help you to understand what had happened or why they said what they said.

What If It All Goes Wrong?

What if the other person gets really angry and defensive and now there is overt hostility between you? Then what?

This was a strong possibility in my situation with Sam, and one I needed to plan for.

I could imagine him saying something like: "That's just how I am…deal with it" or "Lighten up…I was just joking…"?

I could imagine him getting angry and defensive and refusing to talk about it.

So what if THAT happens.

Now what?

Considering the possibility that it could all go wrong requires some finesse.

We don't want to get fixated on worst case scenarios for our upcoming difficult conversation, because all that will do is create unnecessary stress. Why make ourselves miserable about something that hasn't happened and might not happen?

We also don't want to do this because the natural response to replaying worst case scenarios is to get really upset over them.

It's (unfortunately) natural to add commentary like:

> "How dare she act like such a jerk!!!"
>
> "I hate it when Joe does that!!!"
>
> "Of course Sally is going to deny it and then..."

Think of times you've done that and how it affects your emotional state.

You end up feeling angry, even more anxious about having the conversation, and even resentful towards the other person, and...IT HASN'T EVEN HAPPENED!

They haven't said ANY of that to you...YOU did!

So, we don't want to imagine the worst case scenario and do THAT.

What we DO want to do is use it to create an effective strategy for dealing with the worst case scenario and other non-optimal outcomes.

This kind of planning not only prepares us to perform well in difficult situations, it also reduces our anxiety. Because we've "done our homework" and have considered a number of outcomes and how we would respond, we have an increased feeling of mastery and the attitude: "Whatever happens...I'll be ready."

We want to think of alternative possibilities because we don't want our plan dependent on the other person acting exactly like we had hoped. While we can't plan for every possible response they might have, we

CAN consider likely ones and how we might deal with them, rather than being caught off guard with no idea of how to respond.

What If Sam Blows Me Off?

I started to consider responses Sam might have other than "Hey Dave.... thanks for sharing. I'll never do that again..."

I considered the likely possibility that Sam would get defensive and say something like: "That's just how I am...deal with it" or "Lighten up...I was just joking..."

If he were to say that, I was clear I wouldn't simply think "Well...at least I tried" and slink away. I was clear that I would not tolerate this behavior.

I was clear I would not tolerate that behavior, but...at that point, I had no idea "not tolerating it" meant.

What would that actually look and sound like in real life?

What would I tell him I would do if he does it again?

I decided I would say something like: "OK...you may think it's OK, but it isn't OK with me. So...if it happens again, we're going to meet with Claire (our mutual supervisor)."

Here's the problem: Claire was unlikely to support me on this.

I had discovered this unpleasant reality after reaching out to a colleague who had been acting as an informal mentor to me during these early months working there. When I told her what had happened, and asked her for her perspective and recommendations, she told me she had a similar unpleasant interaction with Sam and had brought it up to Claire, who was also her supervisor.

When she did, Claire said "Oh…that's just Sam being Sam."

Okay….

Given Claire's response to my colleague, it was clear that I would need to talk with her before asking her to intervene, if and when Sam dismissed my request and acted out again.

This part of my strategy brought up another issue. What if Claire wasn't interested in supporting me?

What if she said "Oh…that's just Sam…" just like she had done to my colleague?

I was clear that I would not continue to work there if Sam was allowed to behave this way, but…I was also acutely aware of how much I needed the job and how difficult it would be to find a replacement job that payed as well.

Thus, I wanted to think carefully about how I could best persuade Claire to back me up, given that she was not likely to do so without some convincing.

How Do You Manage Up When Your Boss Isn't Likely to Care?

When managing up, it's important to see the situation from your manager's perspective.

It's easy to be self-focused in these situations and make our request very me-centric, listing all the reasons why we want what we want. It takes a bit of discipline to shift perspective and ask:

- "What's important to them and how does my request relate to that?"
- "How does this thing I want help them get what they want?"
- "How can I frame my request or my position in terms that are relevant to them?"

When we look beyond our own desires and try to truly understand the desires of the person we wish to influence, we are far more likely to be heard.

Keeping this in mind, here's what I came up with:

> "If we tolerate managers—or any employee—mistreating others, then our current initiative—that of creating

> a more respectful, positive workplace—would be seen as a farce. If we admonished employees to treat each other well and didn't address disrespectful behavior when it did arise, employees would understandably lose respect for our management team and message."

Management was also concerned about the company's low employee satisfaction scores (this was before employee engagement was a "thing") and managers had been discussing how to improve it. I decided I would also point out that allowing toxic behavior to continue would obviously not help their efforts.

I also decided that, if necessary, I would play the "If it continues and is not addressed, I will need to start looking for an employer that doesn't tolerate this behavior" card.

In essence, if nothing else worked, I would use the "It's either him or me" ultimatum, said in a gentler way.

As I considered this "nuclear option," I was painfully aware of my weak bargaining position.

You see, Sam's position would be much harder to fill than mine, as this was during a time when it was almost impossible to find IT talent. Thus, even if I was technically in the right, I could imagine Claire choosing Sam over me, because he would be far harder to replace.

So you can see that I didn't have a particularly strong bargaining position to work from. I share this because I want you to know that I understand that, by definition, difficult conversations involve making difficult, and sometimes scary, choices. I also want to emphasize that I am not suggesting you do something I haven't been willing to do.

As I thought about how I would word my position if it came to an "It's him or me" moment, I considered the fact that Claire was a very high D in the DiSC profile—D as in Driver, Director, or Dominant.

High Ds have strong, often forceful, personalities and need to be in charge. If their Alpha status is challenged—especially if they hold a position of power—High Ds will very likely go into overdrive to show you that THEY are the boss, THEY are the dominant one in the relationship.

I would need to keep Claire's High D personality in mind while thinking how to get the "It's him or me" message across in a low-key, non-threatening, non-aggressive way. I would need to communicate clearly that I recognized she was in charge.

Making this clear doesn't require groveling or self-deprecation. It can be accomplished by saying something like:

> *"I know you're the boss and it's your decision about how to handle this, not mine, but I also want to be forthright about where I stand on this...if Sam continues to say those kinds of things with impunity, I'm going to be looking for a new job. I don't want to have to do that, but I also am not OK with being treated that way. I'm not saying this as an ultimatum, but just to put all my cards on the table."*

If I said this, Claire STILL might get defensive and shift to steamroller mode, but that's simply a reality of bringing up difficult issues or saying difficult things. You can influence, but not control, how the other person responds.

All you can control is:

- How well you prepare (or IF you prepare).

- Whether you do the work, and have the skills, to shift into a productive emotional and mental state.

- The words you choose to bring up the issue.

- The voice tone, volume, and other aspects of your vocal and non-verbal delivery.

Doesn't All This Worst Case Scenario Thinking Just Add To Your Stress?

My thinking through how I might address the Sam issue with Claire might seem premature. It might seem like I was adding unnecessary angst to an already stressful situation. I mean, I hadn't even talked with Sam yet, and here I am thinking about what could be an even more challenging conversation with my supervisor?

While I don't believe it's helpful to ruminate on potentially stressful conversations far out in the future, I do believe it's important to reflect on "What ifs."

Doing so not only helps you feel more prepared and respond more effectively if the situation does arise, but also shapes your choices and planning for the immediate conversation.

So in this instance, if Sam responded by saying "Oh lighten up…I'm just kidding," I wanted to be ready for that.

In anticipating that possible outcome, I needed to consider whether it was a viable option to say to Sam ""OK…you may think it's OK but it isn't to me…If this happens again, I'm going to insist on a meeting with Claire."

Even though I didn't have a whole lot of faith that Claire would support me, I believed she might, so I would have the "OK…you may think it's OK…" response ready if needed.

That being said, if I were coaching someone in this situation, I would recommended they do a brief examination of how they might deal with Claire, but not spend much time drilling down into the tactics, since that was only a hypothetical at that point. What was NOT hypothetical was the upcoming conversation with Sam, so that's where 99% of my attention needed to be.

It's Game On...

Now it's the following morning. I feel as ready as I can possibly be. I am in an alert, curious, ready-to-be-my-best-self state. I know what outcome I want, but am not overly attached to it. In other words, I've acknowledged to myself it might not go the way I hope, and so be it.

I walk out onto the call center floor and go to Sam's cubicle.

He's there.

My first goal is to get him to an office where we can talk in private. Even though few people are around this early in the morning, I don't want to turn our conversation into a spectator sport.

I walk up to Sam and say: "Hey Sam…do you have a minute to talk?"

Because we had no history of bad blood between us, no overt conflict, I felt comfortable with that as the initial request. If we had overt ill will between us, I would have chosen a different opener.

Imagine you are Sam and there's a history of conflict and tension between us, and I ask you "Do you have a minute to talk?" or "Do you have a minute to talk about something?"

Wouldn't you be thinking "Great…NOW what?" and instantly be on guard?

In that state, you would be far less likely to be open to what I had to say or perceive it as anything but an attack.

I share this because getting good at bringing up difficult issues, requires being mindful of word choice and awareness of what phrases can trigger an unwanted emotional reaction.

If we'd had a history of overt conflict, I might have said "Hey Sam… can I run something by you and get your perspective on it?"

Put yourself in Sam's shoes, once again. If I asked you that, you would probably feel open and curious. I was asking for your help and input.

Now, also notice that framing my request for a conversation that way is truthful.

I DO want his perspective.

I DO want to hear his point of view.

So it's not a "bait and switch" way of bringing up a difficult issue. I just want to mention that because being skillful in phrasing things that won't trigger defensiveness is NOT about being disingenuous or dishonest.

In response to my asking him if he had a minute to talk, Sam says "Sure…"

I suggest we go into an empty office nearby.

It's game on…

In a neutral tone of voice, I say something like:

"Hey Sam...I don't know if you remember in yesterday's meeting when you said 'That idea stinks and so do you' to me....I'm sure you were trying to be funny...but being on the receiving end of that...it didn't feel funny...so I was curious what you meant by that."

Let's dissect my opening, my Declaration/Invitation

"Hey Sam...I don't know if you remember in yesterday's meeting when you said 'That idea stinks and so do you' ...."

Notice, I got right to the point. I didn't beat around the bush. If we start off a potentially difficult conversation with a long lead up, the person might start wondering "What are you talking about? What are you getting at?" and begin to feel confused, and then irritated.

Also, if we go on and on, the person can start to feel like they aren't being invited into a dialogue, but instead are being talked at...because they ARE being talked at.

Notice also that I stated as verbatim as possible what he had said to me.

We want to do that as best we can for two reasons:

1. So the person knows exactly what we're talking about.

2. Because hearing one's own words from someone else can often help people appreciate the impact far better than paraphrasing the gist of what they said or merely telling them how you were affected by it.

One of the most important criteria for an effective Declaration/ Invitation is that it be clear and concrete, because being clear and concrete helps prevent confusion.

When people are confused about what we're saying--especially when they are getting negative feedback or being confronted—they can start to feel helpless: "OK…I get it that you're upset with me or I did something wrong, but I have no idea what it is that you're unhappy about…. so how am I supposed to do something about it?"

Feeling helpless is obviously stressful, which makes it more likely the person will lash out.

"…I'm sure you were trying to be funny…"

OK, this was a bit of a stretch. I WASN'T sure he was only trying to be funny, but it WAS possible and in most situations, I think it's best to give people the benefit of the doubt rather than assume malicious intent. We want that from others, so why wouldn't they want it from us? From a purely tactical point of view, you're much less likely to trigger defensiveness if you indicate you are giving them the benefit of the doubt, than if you attribute their behavior to negative intent.

"…but being on the receiving end of that…it didn't feel too funny…"

This is the level of openness and vulnerability I settled on during the preparation stage. As I mentioned earlier, I had wrestled with the issue of how open and vulnerable I wanted to be with Sam, given his past behavior. This phrase "speaks my truth" and communicates how I experienced his remarks, but in a way that was not overly transparent or vulnerable.

At the risk of getting into the linguistic weeds for a moment, notice I used the third person—"It didn't feel too funny"—versus the first person—"I felt uncomfortable" or "I was bothered by that". When we use third person, it depersonalizes the message a bit. While using first person fosters openness and closeness when sharing with a partner or close friend, if you DON'T want to be as open with someone or vulnerable, third person helps to achieve that.

Notice the phrase "...but being on the receiving end of that...it didn't feel too funny**...**" doesn't include potentially emotionally charged words that could trigger a defensive reaction.

For instance, when asking seminar participants how they might bring up the issue to Sam, sometimes people will say "I would say 'I was really offended by your comment'."

I don't recommend using the word "offended", because there's a lot of baggage around the word "offended," at least in the American culture where being offended is a national pastime and seems to be a source of pride for many.

When people use the phrase "I'm offended by that," the subtext in our culture is: "That's an inappropriate thing to say, you need to apologize to me so I can move on, and you should never say that again."

Because we've been socialized to believe that when someone says they were offended by something we said or did, it means we are at fault, hearing "I'm offended by that" can easily trigger defensiveness. While there might be situations where saying "I was offended" could be useful, I recommend avoiding this overused phrase—and life position—if at all possible.

"...so I was curious what you meant by that?"

Now, to be honest, I can't remember if this was the exact Invitation I used, but if I had to do it over again, I would have said this or I might have said "...so I'm curious about where you were coming from when you said that."

Why Did I Choose This for My Declaration/Invitation?

Let's deconstruct my Declaration/Invitation because there are several key principles to keep in mind about this Invitation—and Invitations in general.

Get to the Invitation As Quickly As Possible

First, notice I got to the Invitation as quickly as possible. I didn't do a long drawn out Declaration for the reasons stated earlier.

My only caveat is that you DO want to use enough words in the Declaration to explain what you want to talk about. Otherwise, the conversation begins with the person being confused about what you are talking about. Confusion leads to the feeling of helplessness, which can trigger anger and aggression. This is because at a primal, unconscious level, helplessness triggers fear, and fear often triggers aggression. Think of a cornered animal and the old saying "the best defense is a good offense." Aggression and the crazed power that can come out of angry, fearful state can sometimes be the difference between life and death when an animal is cornered.

We will talk more about this later, when we briefly delve into what happens to the human brain when people feel confused, frustrated, threatened, or significantly stressed, and how that affects what we need to do to engage people in constructive conversations.

Use a Welcoming Voice Tone

Second, while you can't tell from the written version of this, I was conscious of delivering the Invitation in a low-key tone of voice that conveyed my genuine curiosity and bafflement. I purposely didn't put an edge on my voice or a "WTF was THAT about?" tone.

Think of when people have brought up issues with you and they had a frustrated, exasperated, angry, or just plain hard edge to their voice and how that instantly put you off.

Or maybe you can think of times you've done that as a way to communicate "I'm really upset" or "What you did is REALLY not OK."

Sometimes because we are afraid of being too verbally direct in expressing our displeasure, we opt instead for letting our voice tone convey our displeasure. Unfortunately, doing so typically just triggers a negative reaction.

This is in part because the same parts of the brain that process voice tone and vocal delivery—called prosody—also process emotions and helps to create our emotional response. That's why "how you say it" is just as important, if not more important than, "what you say."

Because of this, it's important to be mindful of our voice tone and make it as non-threatening and welcoming as possible.

Be Mindful of Word Choice

Third, I didn't include any melodramatic words to my message, like "...so I was wondering...what could you have *possibly* meant by that?"

I also didn't include judgments in my Invitation as sometimes people in my seminars do.

I remember one woman at a seminar offering this as her recommended Invitation: "So...I'm wondering what made you think that what you said to me was appropriate?"

Ouch.

I can empathize with her sentiments. I certainly wondered how in the world Sam could think any of the verbal attacks he had made on people were appropriate. However, asking this question would obviously trigger instant defensiveness.

Watch Out for Judgmental Language... No Matter How Warranted

I've also had other people in seminars say they would recommend starting off the conversation with this Declaration: "I thought what you said to me in yesterday's meeting was really inappropriate..." Others have suggested: "I wanted to talk with you about your comments to me yesterday, which were very unprofessional..."

Now again, even though Sam's remarks *were* inappropriate and unprofessional, starting off with those judgments would have virtually guaranteed a defensive, aggressive retort.

So, when you're planning your Declaration/Invitation, make sure you strip out judgments, no matter how justified you might feel they are, unless you're engaging someone in a performance review conversation which requires you to evaluate their behavior. That being said, you can still give someone negative feedback or say their behavior is unacceptable without judging the person as a human being.

One of the ways I've done this is say "I was really taken aback when you said…" Notice that's stating MY experience, it is not labeling or characterizing the other person's behavior in any specific way.

For more information on how to create an effective Declaration/ Invitation, go to: HumanNatureAtWork.com/cc-worksheet.

Sam Responds

After I say: "Hey Sam…I don't know if you remember in yesterday's meeting when you said 'Your idea stunk and so do you'….I'm sure you were trying to be funny…but being on the receiving end of that…it didn't feel too funny…so I was curious what you meant by that," I wait for his response.

His response stuns me.

"Wow…I don't even remember saying that. Thanks for bringing it up."

He pauses and then says "Yeah…I really appreciate your bringing it to my attention…I take pride in being a professional and I would hate to think I would say something that would come across as unprofessional."

Can you imagine how dumbfounded I was by *that* response?

First, I was surprised—albeit pleasantly—that he didn't say "Oh…I was just kidding" or some other immature remark.

Second, his "I don't even remember saying that" was a good reminder of the truism "It's better to assume ignorance than malice."

I continually have to remind myself of this over the years.

When someone's behavior seems so overtly unkind or incomprehensibly rude, it's so easy to "explain" it to ourselves in terms of malicious intent, rather than "they spoke without thinking."

Consider the phrase "What a thoughtless thing to say!" It's very possible that they did *literally speak without thinking.*

Third, I found the part about taking pride in being a professional darkly amusing.

If I didn't have control over my Inside Voice, I would have blurted out: "You're kidding...right?"

Was He Really Telling the Truth?

While I was surprised at the time, and for a long time afterwards, that he wasn't even aware of making those comments, now I am not so surprised. In the years following my conversation with Sam, I've experienced, and had friends tell me about times they've experienced, people making thoughtless remarks, who, when asked about why they said what they did, honestly had no recollection of saying what they said, let alone *why*.

Now, you might be thinking "Well...they're just not admitting it. They're just lying."

I have three thoughts about this:

1. In the case of Sam, he seemed genuinely shocked and genuinely appreciative that I shared with him what he had said.

2. Even if the person pretends not to know what you're referring to, your bringing it up lets them know that if they do such a thing in the future, you will confront them. That alone might be a deterrent to a repeat performance.

3. Whether a person tells you the truth or lies, is outside your control. You can, though, *influence* their choice to tell the truth, or lie, by how non-threatening you are when you bring up the issue.

If you approach them in an accusatory, judging, or scolding manner, you will likely trigger a protective response. By bringing up the issue in a way that communicates "I am here for a candid, respectful conversation," you can influence their willingness to speak honestly and unguardedly.

That being said, you can bring up the issue in a textbook perfect way and they STILL might respond in a less-than-honest or defensive way. That's simply a reality when dealing with people. We can't control how others will respond, we can only influence their response by doing our best to show up and communicate at our best.

What Can We Learn From Sam's Response?

Looking back on his response, it was kind of anticlimactic, given how much angst and effort was involved leading up to this conversation.

That in itself was a great lesson.

Haven't you had conversations like this, where you feared the person would be very difficult to deal with and they weren't?

I try to use those experiences as reminders not to scare myself by playing movies in my head about how unpleasant the person will be when we have the conversation. While I still play these movies in my head when dealing with someone who has a track record of immaturity, I offset it to some degree with the reality-testing reminder that I've had these kinds of conversations in the past and people with a history of acting immaturely CAN respond maturely.

Also, having had a few conversations over the years where I suspected malice, only to discover there was none, I am much better at going into these types of conversations with a "Seek first to understand" attitude and a willingness to give the person the benefit of the doubt.

Where NOT To Go From Here

After Sam said:

> "Wow...I don't even remember saying that...Thanks for bringing it up...yeah...I really appreciate your bringing it to my attention...I take pride in being a professional and I would hate to think I would say something that would come across as unprofessional."

Now what?

Where do I go from here?

First off, what I DON'T want to do is belabor the point by saying "Well...if you WERE trying to put me down or give me a hard time, I hope you realize that wouldn't have been OK with me" or some other warning or ultimatum about a hypothetical situation.

Haven't you had people do that?

They say "Well if you..." followed by some behavior or decision they find unacceptable—and you haven't done, nor would you do—and then follow it with the negative consequence they would mete out to you if you ever did such a thing?

You're thinking "Ah…OK…but I would never do that so why are you bringing it up and threatening me?"

That being said, I'm not a big believer in absolutes, so there may be situations where you want to be ultra-clear about what your response would have been, had your theory been accurate. One situation I could see this in, is if you strongly suspect they weren't telling the truth and you want to be very clear about what you would do or say IF that does happen.

So for example, "OK Jeremy, I'll take your word that you did not look up your girlfriend's medical records on our system. However, I just want to be super clear, because I don't want you to be caught off guard, looking up the medical records of someone you know is a fire-able offense. It's that serious of an ethical violation. Are you clear on that?"

OK, back to Sam.

I actually can't remember what I said after he thanked me and said he would hate to be seen as unprofessional. I can imagine me saying something like:

"I appreciate hearing that…I really want us and the rest of the team to work well together, which is why I wanted to check in with you about this rather than just wonder about it…"

With this line, I am expressing both appreciation for his concern and stating why I brought up the issue. Notice that my reason why was stated as a positive: "I really want us and the rest of the team to work well together."

That's a much friendlier frame than the equally true "negative frame" which was I wanted to make sure that he didn't repeat this behavior.

From this point, I think we did just a bit of chit chat. My guess is I probably switched gears to talking about totally non-threatening topics related to our team.

If Sam had been a friend, I would have wanted to talk more about what happened and my feelings about it. With Sam, doing so would probably have turned a good situation bad.

My reasoning won't come as a surprise to you, especially if you are a woman.

Gauging Someone's Comfort with Open, "Deep" Conversation

Had I delved into issues of relationships and feelings, it would have most likely made Sam feel uncomfortable, since talking about these things is foreign territory for many—if not most—men. Sam was a stereotypical techie, so it would have been even more foreign territory to him.

Because it would have likely felt too raw and intimate of a conversation, and one that he didn't have a lot of experience with, he would have probably gone from feeling anxious and threatened to becoming defensive and aggressive.

I'm not sure of the origin of the following truism, but it's a useful reminder: "When people act threatening, it's because they feel threatened." I once read a version of this truism in a book by Martha Beck, where she wrote: "When people get scared, they act scary."

Given this reality, I chose to not "go there" and end the conversation as quickly as possible and on a high note.

True Confession Time

Okay, I have to admit something before sharing how we ended the conversation.

Sam repeated his concern about having acted inappropriately several times and came across as contrite. Experiencing him shift from acting like a bully to being contrite and apologetic triggered this weird, primitive response in me.

I felt this surge of power and almost elation.

Looking back on my response, it was the response of a warrior standing over a vanquished foe, a foe who had been an oppressor and now the tables had turned.

I felt this urge to further cement my position of having the upper hand.

While it felt strange to have this urge bubble up inside of me, it makes sense from a paleopsychological perspective.

Paleopsychology is a term that refers to hard-wired survival responses and perspectives that are leftovers from our ancient cave-dwelling ancestors.

It's the psychology of our Inner Neanderthal if you will.

These primitive responses originate in the most primitive region of the brain—often called the Reptilian Brain. If your brain is like a modern computer with software that can do amazingly complex tasks, the Reptilian Brain is like a thumb drive loaded with primitive, "survival of the fittest" programs being plugged into a state-of-the art computer.

These programs were "written" hundreds of thousands, and even millions, of years ago for a world very different than the world we live in today. Dr. Paul MacLean named this primitive region of the brain the Reptilian Brain because it resembles modern day reptile brains and because he believed it was similar to reptile brains 200 million years ago.

According to Dr. MacLean and others who built upon his work, these hardwired survival programs include:

- **The drive for power and control**—If you have power and control, you are more likely to survive than if you are powerless and helpless.

- **Feeling helpless or powerless triggers fear which triggers aggression**—In a "law of the jungle," "the strong will survive" world, being helpless means you will soon be dead. Thus, it makes sense that feeling helpless or powerless in a situation would trigger fear at the most primal level. Even when it's not a life or death situation in today's modern world, when people feel helpless or powerless, the Reptilian Brain registers this and activates the survival program of fear aggression.

  If you're a caveman or cavewoman and feel helpless in the face of an attack and you cannot flee, your last, best chance at preventing your demise, is to launch a fury-fueled pre-emptive attack.

> Keep in mind this is not a conscious decision, it's an automatic, hardwired survival response. Now, as you're probably thinking, not everyone demonstrates aggression when afraid. Some exhibit the "flight" survival program as their default, and others exhibit the "freeze" survival program. The key for our purposes is to recognize that fear aggression is a natural, hardwired response to feeling threatened, and therefore a good reason to NOT threaten others by the way we bring up an issue.

Back to Sam and me...

So while on one hand, I had just been very conscious and intentional about bringing up the issue to Sam in a non-threatening, respectful way and monitoring my responses, on the other hand, my Inner Neanderthal reared up its head and wanted to put a spear through my vanquished foe's chest.

The way I wanted to do this was by pointing out all the other times he had mistreated other people.

One of the things I know about myself is that I have a strong desire to try to make the world a kinder, more respectful, thoughtful place. I also have a strong aversion to injustice. So when I witness people being mean or unkind, I want to get them to see the error of their ways.

Part of this comes from a strong teacher archetype. I love sharing things I think will benefit others and will make a difference in the world.

However, "helping" someone see the error of their ways is not often appropriate or welcomed. In fact, unless you have a major level of trust with the other person, you can virtually guarantee your insights will not be received with open arms.

Fortunately, I was able to squelch my Reptilian Brain and Teacher Archetype-fueled desire to share my observations about Sam's ongoing pattern and try to "help" him change his ways. My more rational, logical prefrontal lobe saved the day and reminded me that doing this would undoubtedly ruin the positive interaction we had enjoyed up to this point.

Let's End This Off on a High Note

As I mentioned earlier, I realized that if I prolonged the conversation any longer than was necessary, it would likely bring us into territory that Sam would find too emotionally intimate, and would likely trigger a negative response, undoing the progress we had made.

So to wind things up, I said: "Well…thanks for being willing to talk about this. I really appreciate that."

He responded by saying something like "No man…thank YOU for bringing it to my attention."

We got up and walked out of the office.

Sam never made another one of those comments to me, and I never witnessed him doing that to anyone else, either.

What Can We Learn From This Story?

I like to use this story in my seminars because it speaks to several important points to keep in mind when contemplating "Is it worth having the conversation with this difficult person?"

1. **You just never know** -- Even people with a history of acting immaturely, rudely, or disrespectfully can rise to the occasion when approached in a mature, respectful way. So even situations where you think "there's NO way this is going to have a happy ending"…it just might.

2. **It's SO worth taking the time to prepare** – If I had simply stormed over to Sam's cubicle while roiling with anger, and had confronted him in an aggressive, judgmental way, I can guarantee our conversation would have had a very different outcome. That's why I teach "The Before-You-Have-the-Conversation Moment of Truth will make or break the conversation". The time and effort you put into shifting from a negative to a positive—or at least neutral—emotional state, and thinking through the best way to bring up the issue, will pay *huge* dividends in terms of the conversation going well.

   Sometimes when I say this, a seminar participant will respond "Boy…that's a LOT of work…that's a LOT of time to spend on a single conversation."

Yes it is.

And...it's time well spent.

We can either spend the time up front to make the conversation go well, or the time after it goes badly, trying to repair the damage.

I choose to spend time on the preparation side.

3. **Thoughtless comments and behavior are often just that: spoken or done without thought** – Sam's genuine surprise at hearing what he had said was a nice reminder that people can say unkind and insensitive things without any intended ill will. I've caught myself over the years realizing later that something I said in a conversation might have been misinterpreted. It might have come across as too harsh, dismissing what the other person had said, or had some other negative impact.

   When I've reached out to the person and shared my concern and apologized if it had come across that way, the other person has usually said "Oh...I don't even remember that" or "Oh thanks...no...it didn't come across that way at all" Other times, they've simply said something like: "It did kind of come across that way. I appreciate your noticing and apologizing."

   Reminding ourselves "It's better to assume ignorance than ill will" doesn't just save us from the emotional and physical wear and tear created from working ourselves into self-righteous outrage through assuming we can read other's minds.

   It also keeps us from entering into the conversation with a negative attribution and accompanying negative emotional state. "Negative attribution" means we attribute another person's actions to some negative intention. If we come to the conversation attributing negative intention to their behavior, this will be communicated in our voice tone, word choice, and overall demeanor. They will pick up on this and are likely to respond like most people do when they sense the other person has negative feelings about them or is judging them.

Conversely, if we come with an open mind and an open heart, they are more likely to feel safe enough to talk openly and non-defensively.

A Quick Review and Reminders For Future Courageous Conversations

1. Discharge your anger before having the conversation by venting to a close friend or coach.

2. Ask a wise friend or coach for their perspective, including alternative explanations for the other person's behavior and your possible role in the incident. They will be more rational and unbiased because they are not caught up in the drama.

3. Identify and challenge the stories and explanations you've come up with to explain why the person did what they did. Recognize Mind Reading for what it is: an irrational assumption that our theory about why someone did what they did is just that—a theory. It is not a fact.

4. Think through potential responses from the other person and strategize how you might reply, but challenge yourself if you slip into Fortune Telling and Catastrophizing.

5. As you think of the other person's potential responses and their consequences, ask yourself if you're willing to accept and deal with the potential consequences that are most serious. If you are not sure how realistic the most feared ones are, ask your wise friend or coach.

6. If you decide to bring up the issue, use the following questions to help you come up with a Declaration/Invitation that invites the other person into a productive dialogue, rather than immediately putting them on the defensive:

    a. "How would I feel if someone brought this issue up to me in this way?"

    b. "Am I using the least amount of intensity to make my point?"—In other words, are you using a voice tone and words that communicate respect and goodwill rather than anger, judgment, and/or scolding?

    c. "What approach on my part would be for the Highest Good?"

7. Once you come up with a Declaration/Invitation, run it by your trusted friend or coach for their feedback, and tweak if necessary.

8. If you have the conversation and it doesn't go well, don't use this as evidence that you shouldn't have had the conversation, that there was nothing you could have done to make it work, or that you should avoid having courageous conversations in the future. While it's possible that nothing you or anyone else could have said would have elicited a productive response in the other person, it's far more likely that a more skillful approach on your part would have worked. The key is to learn what "more skillful" would have looked and sounded like. That's where processing what happened with a wise friend or coach comes into play.

Next Steps

1. If you haven't done so already, go to HumanNatureAtWork.com/cc-worksheet and download the worksheet. Use it to come up with your own Declaration/Invitation for whatever conversation or conversations you were thinking of as you read this.

2. If you want to build on what you've learned so far, you can also order the CD "Let's Talk for a Change!" which was recorded at a conference and uses this story as the framework. The talk explores the four components we need to get right when having a courageous conversation. You can find it at HumanNatureAtWork.com.

3. If you are interested in bringing this to your organization, whether facilitated in-house or having me come and speak, email me: David@HumanNatureAtWork.com.

4. If you are interested in coaching, feel free to email me.

Printed in Great Britain
by Amazon

61692839R00050